OCCASION…

The Essence of Islamic Civilization

Ismaʿīl Rājī al Fārūqī

THE INTERNATIONAL INSTITUTE OF ISLAMIC THOUGHT
LONDON · WASHINGTON

P.O. BOX 669, HERNDON, VA 20172, USA
www.iiit.org

LONDON OFFICE
P.O. BOX 126, RICHMOND, SURREY TW9 2UD, UK
www.iiituk.com

978-1-56564-597-4

IMAGES p.7, 8, 24, 26, 27 *iStockphoto*
p.9, 12, 29 *Dr. Anas S. al-Shaikh-Ali*
p.30 *Wikimedia Commons*

Typesetting by Sideek Ali
Cover design by Shiraz Khan

Series Editors
DR. ANAS S. AL-SHAIKH-ALI
SHIRAZ KHAN

Foreword

THE INTERNATIONAL INSTITUTE OF ISLAMIC THOUGHT (IIIT) has great pleasure in presenting Occasional Paper 21 *The Essence of Islamic Civilization* by Ismaʿīl al Fārūqī. It was originally published as chapter four of *The Cultural Atlas of Islam* by Ismaʿīl al Fārūqī and Lois Lamyā' al Fārūqī (1986), and formed part of a monumental and authoritative work presenting the entire worldview of Islam, its beliefs, traditions, institutions, and place in the world. Aside from the map illustrations and two arabesques all other images have been updated and are not those of the original.

Professor Ismaʿīl Rājī al Fārūqī (1921–1986) was a Palestinian-American philosopher, visionary, and an authority in comparative religion. A great contemporary scholar of Islam his scholarship encompassed the whole spectrum of Islamic Studies covering areas such as the study of religion, Islamic thought, approaches to knowledge, history, culture, education, interfaith dialogue, aesthetics, ethics, politics, economics, and science. Without doubt al Fārūqī was one of the great Muslim scholars of the 20th century. In this paper he presents the meaning and message of Islam to the wider world, pointing to *tawḥīd* (the unity of God) as its essence and first determining principle which gives Islamic civilization its identity.

The IIIT, established in 1981, has served as a major center to facilitate serious scholarly efforts based on Islamic vision, values and principles. The Institute's programs of research, seminars and conferences during the last thirty years have resulted in the publication of more than four hundred titles in English and Arabic, many of which have been translated into other major languages.

ANAS S. AL-SHAIKH-ALI
Academic Advisor, IIIT London Office

The Essence of Islamic Civilization

THERE can be no doubt that the essence of Islamic civilization is Islam; or that the essence of Islam is *tawḥīd*, the act of affirming Allah to be the One, absolute, transcendent Creator, Lord and Master of all that is.

These two fundamental premises are self-evident. They have never been doubted by those who belonged to this civilization or participated in it. And only very recently have missionaries, Orientalists, and other interpreters of Islam subjected them to doubt. Whatever their level of education, Muslims are apodictically certain that Islamic civilization does have an essence, that this essence is knowable and capable of analysis or description, that it is *tawḥīd*.[1] Analysis of *tawḥīd* as essence, as first determining principle of Islamic civilization, is the object of this chapter.

Tawḥīd is that which gives Islamic civilization its identity, which binds all its constituents together and thus makes of them an integral, organic body which we call civilization. In binding disparate elements together, the essence of civilization – in this case, *tawḥīd* – impresses them with its own mold. It recasts them so as to harmonize with and mutually support other elements. Without necessarily changing their natures, the essence transforms the elements making up a civilization, giving them their new character as constitutive of that civilization. The range of transformation may vary from slight to radical, depending on how relevant the essence is to the different elements and their functions. This relevance stood out prominently in the minds of Muslim observers of the phenomena of civilization.

That is why they took *tawḥīd* as title to their most important works, and they pressed all subjects under its aegis. They regarded *tawḥīd* as the most fundamental principle which includes or determines all other principles; and they found in it the fountainhead, the primeval source determining all phenomena of Islamic civilization.

Traditionally and simply expressed, *tawḥīd* is the conviction and witnessing that "there is no God but God." This negative statement, brief to the utmost limits of brevity, carries the greatest and richest meanings in the whole of Islam. Sometimes, a whole culture, a whole civilization, or a whole history lies compressed in one sentence. This certainly is the case of the *kalimah* (pronouncement) or *shahādah* (witnessing) of Islam. All the diversity, wealth and history, culture and learning, wisdom and civilization of Islam is compressed in this shortest of sentences "*Lā ilaha illā Allah.*"

Tawḥīd as Worldview

Tawḥīd is a general view of reality, of truth, of the world, of space and time, of human history. As such it comprehends the following principles:

Duality

Reality is of two generic kinds, God and non-God; Creator and creature. The first order has but one member, Allah, the Absolute and Almighty. He alone is God, eternal, Creator, transcendent. Nothing is like unto Him; He remains forever absolutely unique and devoid of partners or associates. The second is the order of space-time, of experience, of creation. It includes all creatures, the world of things, plants and animals, humans, jinn and angels, heaven and earth, paradise and hell, and all their becoming since they came into being. The two orders of Creator and creation are utterly and absolutely disparate as far as their being, or ontology, as well as their existence and careers are concerned. It is forever impossible that the one be united with, fused, confused or diffused into the other. Neither can the Creator be ontologically transformed so as to become the creature, nor can the creature transcend and transfigure itself so as to become in any way or sense the Creator.[2]

Ideationality

The relation between the two orders of reality is ideational in nature. Its point of reference in man is the faculty of understanding. As organ and repository of knowledge, the understanding includes all the gnoseological functions of memory, imagination, reasoning, observation, intuition, apprehension, and so on. All humans are endowed with understanding. Their endowment is strong enough to understand the will of God in either or both of the following ways: when that will is expressed in words, directly by God to man, and when the divine will is deducible through observation of creation.[3]

Teleology

The nature of the cosmos is teleological, that is, purposive, serving a purpose of its Creator, and doing so out of design. The world has not been created in vain, or in sport.[4] It is not the work of chance, a happenstance. It was created in perfect condition. Everything that exists does so in a measure proper to it and fulfills a certain universal purpose.[5] The world is indeed a "cosmos," an orderly creation, not a "chaos." In it, the will of the Creator is always realized. His patterns are fulfilled with the necessity of natural law. For they are innate in the very nature of things. No creature other than man, acts or exists in a way other than what the Creator has ordained for it.[6] Man is the only creature in which the will of God is actualized not necessarily, but with man's own personal consent. The physical and psychic functions of man are integral to nature, and as such they obey the laws pertinent to them with the same necessity as all other creatures. But the spiritual functions, namely, understanding and moral action, fall outside the realm of determined nature. They depend upon their subject and follow his determination. Actualization of the divine will by them is of a qualitatively different value than necessary actualization by other creatures. Necessary fulfillment applies only to elemental or utilitarian values; free fulfillment applies to the moral. However, the moral purposes of God, His commandments to man, do have a base in the physical world, and hence there is a utilitarian aspect to them. But this is not what gives them their distinctive quality, that of being moral. It is precisely the commandments' aspect of being fulfillable in freedom, that is, with the possibility of being violated, that provides the special dignity we ascribe to things "moral."[7]

Capacity of Man and Malleability of Nature

Since everything was created for a purpose – the totality of being no less so – the realization of that purpose must be possible in space and time.[8] Otherwise, there is no escape from cynicism. Creation itself and the processes of space and time would lose their meaning and significance. Without this possibility, *taklīf*, or moral obligation, falls to the ground; and with its fall, either God's purposiveness or His might is destroyed. Realization of the absolute, namely, the divine raison d'être of creation, must be possible in history, that is, within the process of time between creation and the Day of Judgment. As subject of moral action, man must therefore be capable of changing himself, his fellows or society, nature or his environment, so as to actualize the divine pattern, or commandment, in himself as well as in them.[9] As object of moral action, man as well as his fellows and environment must all be capable of receiving the efficacious action of man, the subject. This capacity is the converse of man's moral capacity for action as subject. Without it, man's capacity for moral action would be impossible and the purposive nature of the universe would collapse. Again, there would be no recourse from cynicism. For creation to have a purpose – and this is a necessary assumption if God is God and His work is not a

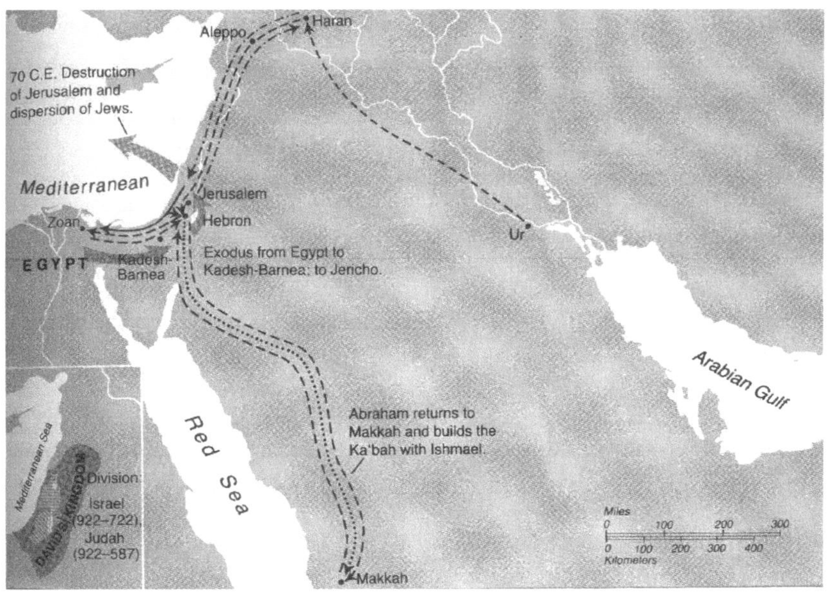

----➤ Abraham's migrations

.........➤ Abraham, Hagar and Ishmael migrate to Makkah

– · –➤ Jacob to Haran; on return his son Joseph is carried off by Arab caravan to Egypt

——➤ Jacob's children to Egypt and return to Hebron

Makkan and Hebrew Origins (1800 B.C.E – 622 C.E.)

meaningless *travail de singe* – creation must be malleable, transformable, capable of changing its substance, structure, conditions, and relations so as to embody or concretize the human pattern or purpose. This is true of all creation, including man's physical, psychic, and spiritual nature. All creation is capable of realization of the ought-to-be, the will or pattern of God, the absolute in this space and in this time.[10]

Responsibility and Judgment

If man stands under the obligation to change himself, his society, and his environment so as to conform with the divine pattern, and is capable of doing so, and if all that is object of his action is malleable

The Makkans and the Hebrews are cousins. Both descend from one ancestor, Abraham or Ibrahim, of Ur in Lower Mesopotamia. Rebelling against the idolatry of his people and escaping miraculously from their judgment against him, Abraham joined the roaming Amurru tribesmen and came to Canaan. He settled his eldest son, Ishmael or Isma'il, in Makkah, where they built the Ka'bah and Isma'il scioned the Makkan tribe of Quraysh. Abraham's other son, Isaac, and his progeny sought to settle in Canaan but could not do so for almost a millennium, during which time they either roamed the area or went to Egypt. They settled in Canaan in the following millennium, but they were torn between assimilation with Canaan and separation from it. Their stay in Canaan ended with destruction, and the survivors dispersed throughout the world during the next two millennia.

and capable of receiving his action and embodying its purpose, then it follows with necessity that he is responsible. Moral obligation is impossible without responsibility or reckoning. Unless man is responsible, and unless he is accountable for his deeds, cynicism becomes once more inevitable. Judgment, or the consummation of responsibility, is the necessary condition of moral obligation, of moral imperativeness. It flows from the very nature of "normativeness."[11] It is immaterial whether reckoning takes place in space-time or at the end of it or both, but it must take place. To obey God, that is, to realize His commandments and actualize His pattern, is to achieve *falāḥ* or success, happiness, and ease. Not to do so, to disobey Him, is to incur punishment, suffering, unhappiness, and the agonies of failure.

Tawḥīd as Essence of Civilization

As the essence of Islamic civilization, *tawḥīd* has two aspects or dimensions: the methodological and the contentual. The former determines the forms of application and implementation of the first principles of the civilization; the latter determines the first principles themselves.

The Methodological Dimension

The methodological dimension includes three principles, namely, unity, rationalism, and tolerance. These determine the form of Islamic civilization, a form that pervades every one of its departments.

UNITY. There is no civilization without unity. Unless the elements constituting a civilization are united, woven, and harmonized with one another, they constitute not a civilization but a hodgepodge conglomeration. A principle unifying the various elements and comprehending them within its framework is essential. Such a principle would transform the mixture of relations of the elements with one another into an orderly structure in which levels of priority or degrees of importance are perceivable. The civilization of Islam places elements in an orderly structure and governs their existence

and relations according to a uniform pattern. In themselves, the elements can be of either native or foreign provenance. Indeed, there is no civilization that has not adopted some elements foreign to it. What is important is that the civilization digest those elements, that is, recast their forms and relations and thus integrate them into its own system. To "in-form" them with its own form is in fact to transform them into a new reality where they exist no more in themselves or in their former dependency, but as integral components of the new civilization in which they have been integrated. It is not an argument against any civilization that it contains such elements; but it is a devastating argument against any civilization when it has merely added foreign elements; when it has done so in disjointed manner, without re-formation, in-formation, or integration. As such, the elements merely co-exist with the civilization. They do not belong organically to it. But if the civilization has succeeded in transforming them and integrating them into its system, the integrating process becomes its index of vitality, of its dynamism and creativity. In any integral civilization, and certainly in Islam, the constitutive elements, whether material, structural, or relational, are all bound by one supreme principle. In Islamic civilization, this supreme principle is *tawḥīd*. It is the ultimate measuring rod of the Muslim, his guide and criterion in his encounter with other religions and civilizations, with new facts or situations. What accords with it is accepted and integrated. What does not is rejected and condemned.

Tawḥīd, or the doctrine of absolute unity, transcendence, and ultimacy of God, implies that only He is worthy of worship, of service. The obedient person lives his life under this principle. He seeks to have all his acts to conform to the pattern, to actualize the divine purpose. His life must therefore show the unity of his mind and will, the unique object of his service. His life will not be a series of events put together helter-skelter, but will be related to a single overarching principle, bound by a single frame which integrates them together into a single unity. His life thus has a single style, an integral form – in short, Islam.

The Qur'an.

RATIONALISM. As methodological principle, rationalism is constitutive of the essence of Islamic civilization. It consists of three rules or laws: first, rejection of all that does not correspond with reality; second, denial of ultimate contradictories; third, openness to new and/or contrary evidence. The first rule protects the Muslim against opinion, that is, against making any untested, unconfirmed claims to knowledge. The unconfirmed claim, the Qur'an declares, is an instance of *ẓann*, or deceptive knowledge,

Mosque of the Prophet in Madīnah.

and is prohibited by God, however slight is its object.[12] The Muslim is definable as the person who claims nothing but the truth. The second rule protects him against simple contradiction on one side, and paradox on the other.[13] Rationalism does not mean the priority of reason over revelation but the rejection of any ultimate contradiction between them.[14] Rationalism studies contradictory theses over and over again, assuming that there must be an aspect that had escaped consideration and that, if taken into account, would expose the contradictory relation. Equally, rationalism leads the reader of revelation – not revelation itself – to another reading, lest an unobvious or unclear meaning may have escaped him which, if reconsidered, would remove the apparent contradiction. Such referral to reason or understanding would have the effect of harmonizing not revelation per se – revelation stands above any manipulation by man! – but the Muslim's human interpretation or understanding of it. It makes his understanding of revelation agree with the cumulative evidence uncovered by reason. Acceptance of the contradictory or paradoxical as ultimately valid appeals only to the weak-of-mind. The intelligent Muslim is a rationalist as he insists on the unity of the two sources of truth, namely, revelation and reason.

The third rule, openness to new or contrary evidence, protects the Muslim against literalism, fanaticism, and stagnation-causing conservatism. It inclines him to intellectual humility. It forces him

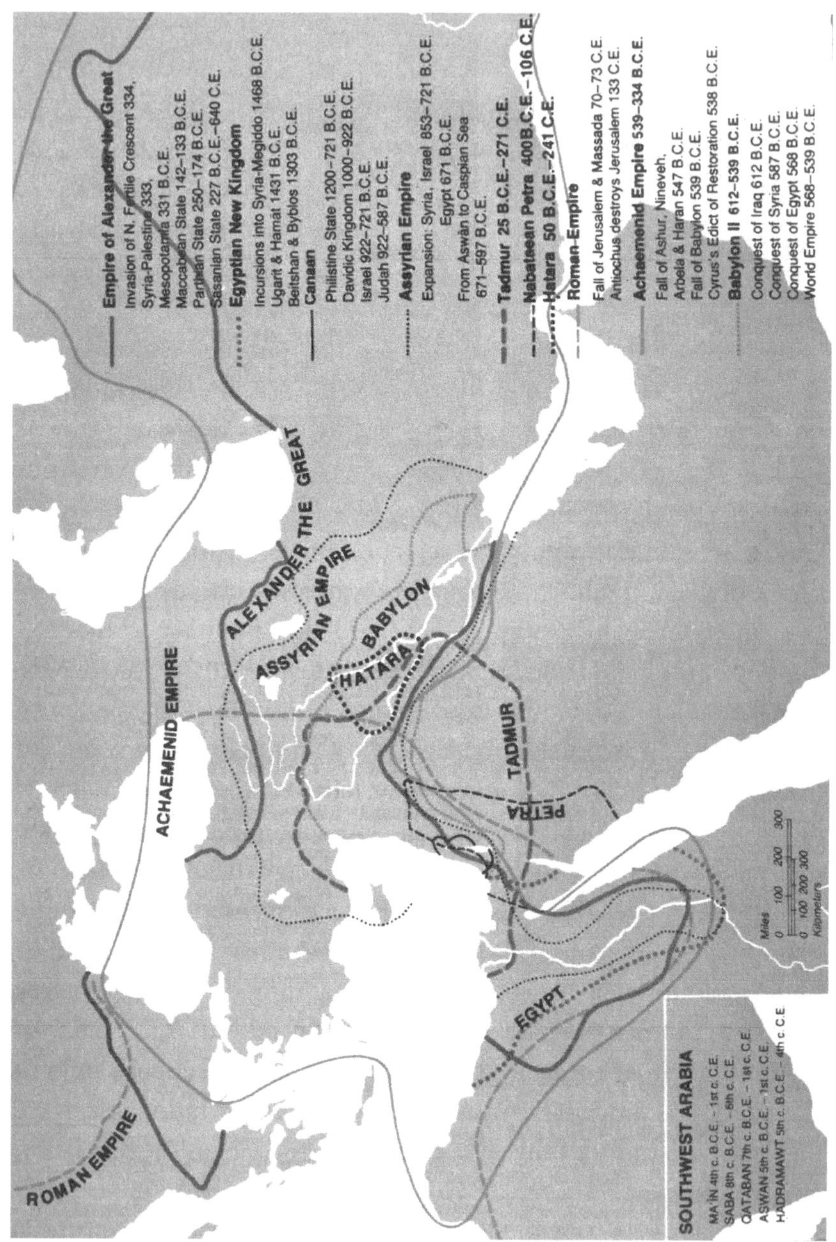

The First Millennium B.C.E.: Power and Turbulence without Idealism.

In the first millennium B.C.E. the Arabian theater saw the rise and fall of five world empires: the Assyrian, Second Babylonian, Persian, Hellenistic, and Roman. None of the twelve states in the area had a sense of mission.

to append to his affirmations and denials the phrase *"Allahu a'lam"*(Allah knows better!). For he is convinced that the truth is bigger than can be totally mastered by him.

As the affirmation of the absolute unity of God, *tawḥīd* is the affirmation of the unity of truth. For God, in Islam, is the truth. His unity is the unity of the sources of truth. God is the Creator of nature whence man derives his knowledge. The object of knowledge are the patterns of nature which are the work of God. Certainly God knows them since He is their author; and equally certainly, He is the source of revelation. He gives man of His knowledge; and His knowledge is absolute and universal. God is no trickster, no malevolent agent whose purpose is to misguide and mislead. Nor does He change His judgment as men do when they correct their knowledge, their will, or their decision. God is perfect and omniscient. He makes no mistakes. Otherwise, He would not be the transcendent God of Islam.

TOLERANCE. As methodological principle, tolerance is the acceptance of the present until its falsehood has been established. Thus, it is relevant to epistemology. It is equally relevant to ethics as the principle of accepting the desired until its undesirableness has been established.[15] The former is called *sa'ah;* the latter, *yusr.* Both protect the Muslim from self-closure to the world, from deadening conservatism. Both urge him to affirm and say yea to life, to new experience. Both encourage him to address the new data with his scrutinizing reason, his constructive endeavor, and thereby to enrich his experience and life, to move his culture and civilization ever forward.

As methodological principle within the essence of Islamic civilization, tolerance is the conviction that God did not leave people without sending them a messenger from among themselves to teach them that there is no God but God and that they owe Him worship and service,[16] to warn them against evil and its causes.[17] In this regard, tolerance is the certainty that all men are endowed with a *sensus communis*, which enables them to know the true religion, to recognize God's will and commandments. Tolerance is the conviction that the diversity of religions is due to history with all its affecting factors, its diverse conditions of space and time, its prejudices, passions, and vested interests. Behind religious diversity stands *al dīn al ḥanīf*, the primordial religion of God with which all men are born before acculturation makes them adherents of this or that religion. Tolerance requires the Muslim to undertake a study of the history of religions with a view to discover within each the primeval endowment of God, which He sent all His apostles at all places and times to teach.[18]

In religion – and there can hardly be anything more important in human relations – tolerance transforms confrontation and reciprocal condemnations between the religions into a cooperative scholarly investigation of the genesis and development of the religions with a view to separating the historical accretions from the original given of revelation. In ethics, the next all important field, *yusr* immunizes the Muslim against any life-denying tendencies and assures him the minimum measure of optimism required to maintain health, balance, and a sense of proportion, despite all the tragedies and afflictions that befall human life. God has assured His creatures that

The Kaʿbah in Makkah.

"with hardship, We have ordained ease *[yusr]*."[19] And as He commanded them to examine every claim and make certain before judging[20] the *uṣūliyyūn* (doctors of jurisprudence) resorted to experimentation before judging as good and evil anything desired that is not contrary to a clear divine injunction.

Both *sa'ah* and *yusr* devolve directly from *tawḥīd* as a principle of the metaphysic of ethics. God, Who created man that he may prove himself worthy in the deed, has made him free and capable of positive action and affirmative movement in the world. To do so, Islam holds, is indeed man's raison d'être.[21]

The Contentual Dimension

TAWḤĪD AS FIRST PRINCIPLE OF METAPHYSICS. To witness that there is no God but God is to hold that He alone is the Creator Who gave to everything its being, Who is the ultimate Cause of every event, and the final End of all that is, that He is the First and the Last. To enter into such witnessing in freedom and conviction, in conscious understanding of its content, is to realize that all that surrounds us, whether things or events, all that takes place in the natural, social, or psychic fields, is the action of God, the fulfillment of one or another of His purposes. Once made, such realization becomes second nature to man, inseparable from him during all his waking hours. One then lives all the moments of one's life under its shadow. And where man recognizes God's commandment and action in every object and event, he follows the divine initiative because it is God's. To observe it in nature is to do natural science.[22] For the divine initiative in nature is none other than the immutable laws with which God had endowed nature.[23] To observe the divine initiative in one's self or in one's society is to pursue the humanities and the social sciences.[24] And if the whole universe itself is really the unfolding or fulfillment of these laws of nature, which are the commandments of God and His will, then the universe is, in the eye of the Muslim, a living theater set in motion by God's command. The theater itself, as well as all it includes, is explicable in these terms. The unization of God means therefore that He is the Cause of everything, and that none else is so.

Of necessity, then, *tawḥīd* means the elimination of any power operative in nature beside God, whose eternal initiative are the immutable laws of nature. But this is tantamount to denying any initiative in nature by any power other than that which is innate in nature, such as magic, sorcery, spirits, and any theurgical notion of arbitrary interference into the processes of nature by any agency. Therefore, *tawḥīd* means the profanization of the realms of nature, their secularization. And that is the absolutely first condition of a science of nature. Through *tawḥīd*, therefore, nature was separated from the gods and spirits of primitive religion. *Tawḥīd* for the first time made it possible for the religio-mythopoeic mind to outgrow itself, for the sciences of nature and civilization to develop with the blessing of a religious worldview that renounced once and for all any association of the sacred with nature. *Tawḥīd* is the opposite of superstition or myth, the enemies of natural science and

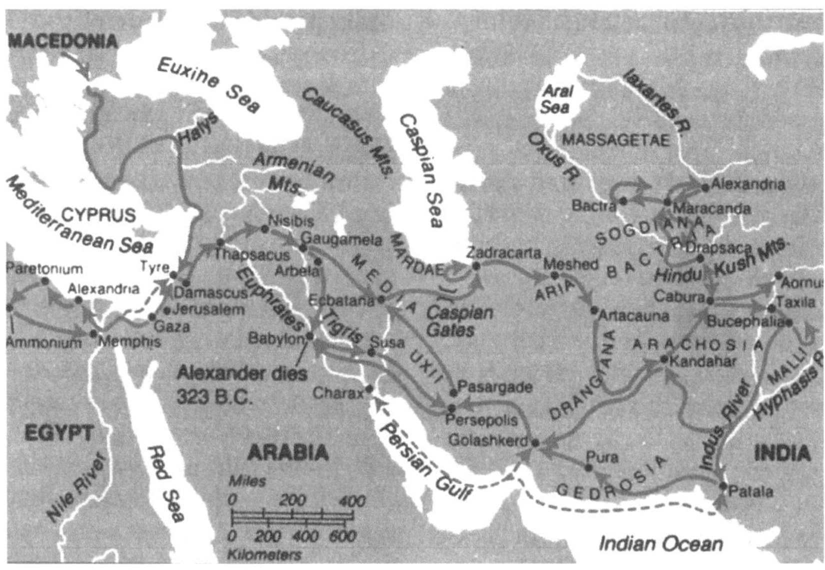

The Campaigns of Alexander the Great.

civilization. For *tawḥīd* gathers all the threads of causality and returns them to God rather than to occult forces. In so doing, the causal force operative in any event or object is organized so as to make a continuous thread whose parts are causally – and hence empirically – related to one another. That the thread ultimately refers to God demands that no force outside of it interferes with the discharge of its causal power or efficacy. This in turn presupposes the linkages between the parts to be causal, and subjects them to empirical investigation and establishment. That the laws of nature are the inimitable patterns of God means that God operates the threads of nature through causes. Only causation by another cause that is always the same constitutes a pattern. This constancy of causation is precisely what makes its examination and discovery – and hence, science – possible. Science is none other than the search for such repeated causation in nature, for the causal linkages constitutive of the causal thread are repeated in other threads. Their establishment is the establishment of the laws of nature. It is the prerequisite for subjecting the causal forces of nature to control and engineering, the necessary condition for man's usufruct of nature.

TAWḤĪD AS FIRST PRINCIPLE OF ETHICS. *Tawḥīd* affirms that the unique God created man in the best of forms to the end of worshipping and serving Him.[25] This means that man's whole existence on earth has as its purpose the obedience of God, the fulfillment of His command. *Tawḥīd* also affirms that this purpose consists in man's vice-gerency for God on earth.[26] For, according to the Qur'an, God has invested man with His trust, a trust which heaven and earth were incapable of carrying and from which they shied away with terror.[27] The divine trust is the fulfillment of the ethical part of the divine will, whose very nature requires that it be realized in freedom, and man is the only creature capable of doing so. Wherever the divine will is realized with the necessity of natural law, the realization is not moral, but elemental or utilitarian. Only man is capable of realizing it under the possibility of doing or not doing so at all, or doing the very opposite or anything in between. It is this exercise of human freedom regarding obedience to God's commandment that makes fulfillment of the command moral.

Tawḥīd affirms that God, being beneficent and purposive, did not create man in sport, or in vain. He endowed him with the senses, with reason and understanding, made him perfect – indeed, breathed into him of His spirit[28] – to prepare him to perform this great duty.

Such great duty is the cause for the creation of man. It is the final end of human existence, man's definition, and the meaning of his life and existence on earth. By virtue of it, man assumes a cosmic function of tremendous importance. The cosmos would not be itself without that higher part of the divine will which is the object of human moral endeavor. And no other creature in the cosmos can substitute for man in this function. Man is the only cosmic bridge by which the moral – and hence higher – part of the divine will may enter the realm of space-time and become history.

The responsibility or obligation (*taklīf*) laid down upon man exclusively knows no bounds. It comprehends the whole universe. All mankind is object of man's moral action; all earth and sky are his theater, his *matériel*. He is responsible for all that takes place in the universe, in every one of its remotest corners. For man's *taklīf* or obligation is universal, cosmic. It comes to end only on the Day of Judgment.

Taklīf, Islam affirms, is the basis of man's humanity, its meaning, and its content. Man's acceptance of this burden puts him on a higher level than the rest of creation, indeed, than the angels. For only he is capable of accepting responsibility. It constitutes his cosmic significance. A world of difference separates this humanism of Islam from other humanisms. Greek civilization, for instance, developed a strong humanism which the West has taken as a model since the Renaissance. Founded upon an exaggerated naturalism, Greek humanism deified man, as well as his vices. That is why the Greek was not offended by representing his gods as cheating and plotting against one another, as committing adultery, theft, incest, aggression, jealousy and revenge, and other acts of brutality. Being part of the very stuff of which human life is made, such acts and passions were claimed to be as natural as the perfections and virtues. As nature, both were thought to be equally divine, worthy of contemplation in their aesthetic form, of adoration – and of emulation by man of whom the gods were the apotheosis. Christianity, on the other hand, was in its formative years reacting to this very Greco-Roman humanism. It went to the opposite extreme of debasing man through "original sin" and declaring him a "fallen creature," a "*massa peccata*."[29]

The degrading of man to the level of an absolute, universal, innate, and necessary state of sin from which it is impossible for any human ever to pull himself up by his own effort was the logical prerequisite if God on High was to incarnate Himself, to suffer, and die in atonement for man's sinfulness. In other words, if a redemption has to take place by God, there must be a predicament so absolute that only God could pull man out of it. Thus human sinfulness was absolutized in order to make it "worthy" of the Crucifixion of God. Hinduism classified mankind into castes, and assigned the majority of mankind to the nethermost classes – of "untouchables" if they are native to India, or *malitcha*, the religiously

Basmalah in mirrored symmetrical design. [Photograph by L. al Fārūqī.]

unclean or contaminated of the rest of the world. For the lowest as well as for the others, there is no rise to the superior, privileged caste of Brahmins in this life; such mobility is possible only after death through the transmigration of souls. In this life, man necessarily belongs to the caste in which he is born. Ethical striving is of no consequence whatever to its subject as long as he is alive in this world. Finally, Buddhism judged all human and other life in creation as endless suffering and misery. Existence itself, it held, is evil and man's only meaningful duty is to seek release from it through discipline and mental effort.

The humanism of *tawḥīd* alone is genuine. It alone respects man as man and creature, without either deification or vilification. It alone defines the worth of man in terms of his virtues, and begins its assessment of him with a positive mark for the innate endowment God has given all men in preparation for their noble task. It alone defines the virtues and ideals of human life in terms of the very contents of natural life, rather than denying them, thus making its humanism life-affirmative as well as moral.

TAWḤĪD AS FIRST PRINCIPLE OF AXIOLOGY. *Tawḥīd* affirms that God has created mankind that men may prove themselves morally worthy by their deeds.[30] As supreme and ultimate Judge, He warned that all men's actions will be reckoned[31]; that their authors will be rewarded for the good deeds and punished for the evil.[32] *Tawḥīd* further affirms that God has placed man on earth that he may colonize it,[33] that is, that he may strike out on its trails, eat of its fruits, enjoy its goodness and beauty, and cause it and himself to prosper.[34] This is world-affirmation: to accept the world because it is innocent and good, created by God and ordered by Him for human use. Indeed, everything in the world, including the sun and the moon, is subservient to man. All creation is a theater in which man is to perform his ethical action and thereby implement the higher part of the divine will. Man is responsible for satisfying his instincts and needs, and every individual is responsible for the same satisfaction for all men. Man is obliged to develop the human resources of all men to the highest possible degree, that full use may be made of all their natural endowments. He is obliged to transform the whole earth into productive orchards and beautiful gardens. He may in the process explore the sun and the moon if necessary.[35] Certainly he must discover and learn the patterns of nature, of the human psyche, of society. Certainly he ought to industrialize and develop the world if it is eventually to become the garden where the word of God is supreme.

Such world affirmation is truly creative of civilization. It generates the elements out of which civilizations are made, as well as the social forces necessary for its growth and progress. *Tawḥīd* is anti-monkery, anti-isolation, anti-world-denial, and anti-asceticism.[36] On the other hand, world affirmation does not mean unconditional acceptance of the world and nature as they are. Without a principle to check man's implementation or realization, affirmation of the world and nature may run counter to itself by the exaggerated pursuit of any one value, element, or force, or group of them, to the exclusion of all others. Balancing and disciplining man's pursuit so that it results in harmonious realization of all values, under the priority system properly belonging to them, rather than under any haste, passion, zeal, or blindness of man, is a necessary prerequisite. Without it, the pursuit may wreck itself in either tragedy or superficiality, or may unleash some truly demonic force. Greek civilization, for instance, exaggerated its pursuit of the world. It asserted that all that is in nature is unconditionally good and hence worthy of pursuit and realization. Hence, it declared all that is actually desired, the object of a real interest, to be *ipso facto* good, on the grounds that desire itself, being natural, is good. That nature often contradicts itself, that and the pursuits of such desires or elements of nature may counter one another, did not have enough appeal to warrant a revision of the first assumption. The need for a supernatural

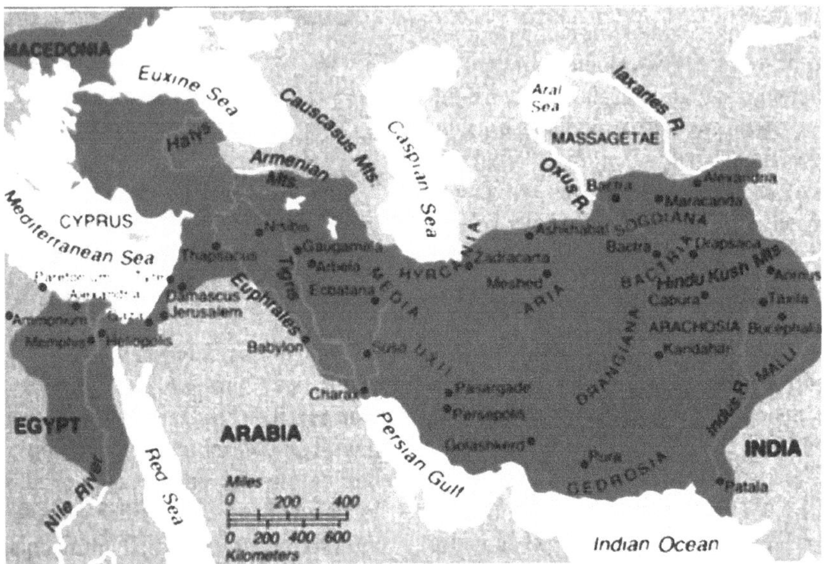

The Empire of Alexander the Great.

principle overarching all the tendencies and desires of nature, and in terms of which their contradictions and differences may be understood, must be recognized. But instead of realizing this truth, Greek civilization was too intoxicated with the beauty of nature per se and regarded the tragic outcome of naturalism itself natural. Since the Renaissance, modern Western civilization has paid the highest regard for tragedy. Its zeal for naturalism took it to the extreme of accepting nature without morality as a supernatural condition. Since the struggle of Western man has been against the Church and all that it represents, the progress of man in science was conceived as a liberation from its clutches. Hence, it was extremely hard even to conceive of world-affirmation or naturalism as attached to normative threads stretching from an a priori, noumenal, absolute source. Without such threads, naturalism is bound to end up in self-contradiction, in conflicts within itself that are *ex hypothesi* insoluble. The Olympus community could not live with itself in harmony and had to destroy itself. Its world-affirmation was in vain.

Calligraphy design (eight Allah repetitions). [Photograph by L. al Fārūqī.]

The guarantee of world-affirmation, which secures it to produce a balanced, permanent, self-redressing civilization, is morality. Indeed, true civilization is nothing but world-affirmation disciplined by an a priori, or supernatural, morality whose inner content or values are not inimical to life and the world, to time and history, to reason. Such morality is furnished by *tawḥīd* alone among the ideologies known to man.

TAWḤĪD AS FIRST PRINCIPLE OF SOCIETISM. *Tawḥīd* asserts that "this ummah of yours is a single ummah whose Lord is God. Therefore, worship and serve Him."[37] *Tawḥīd* means that the believers are indeed a single brotherhood, whose members mutually love one another in God, who counsel one another to do justice and be patient[38]; who cling together without exception to the rope of God and do not separate from one another[39]; who reckon with one another, enjoining what is good and prohibiting what is evil[40]; who, finally, obey God and His Prophet.[41]

The vision of the *ummah* is one; so is the feeling or will, as well as the action. The *ummah* is an order of humans consisting of a tripartite consensus of mind, heart, and arm. There is consensus in their thought, in their decision, in their attitude and character, and in their arms. It is a universal brotherhood which knows neither color nor ethnic identity. In its purview, all men are one, measurable only in terms of piety.[42] If any one of its members acquires a new knowledge, his duty is to teach it to the others. If any one acquires food or comfort, his duty is to share them with the others. If any one achieves establishment, success, and prosperity, his duty is to help the others do likewise.[43]

There is hence no *tawḥīd* without the *ummah*. The *ummah* is the medium of knowledge, of ethics, of the caliphate (vice-gerency) of man, of world-affirmation. The *ummah* is a universal order comprehending even those who are not believers. It is an order of peace, a *Pax Islamica*, forever open to all those individuals and groups who accept the principle of the freedom to convince and to be convinced of the truth, who seek a world order in which ideas, goods, wealth, or human bodies are free to move. The *Pax Islamica* is an international order far surpassing the United Nations, that child of yesteryear, aborted and warped by the principles of the nation-state and the dominion of the "big powers," both of which are constitutive of it. These principles are, in turn, based upon "national sovereignty" as it has evolved in the ideological history of Europe since the Reformation and the demise of the ideal of the universal community the Church had so far half-heartedly carried. But national sovereignty is ultimately based on axiological and ethical relativism.

The United Nations is successful if it fulfills the negative role of preventing or stopping war between the members. Even then, it is an impotent order since it has no army except when the Security Council's "big power" members agree to provide it ad hoc. *Per contra*, the *Pax Islamica* was laid down in a permanent constitution by the Prophet in Madīnah in the first days of the *Hijrah*. He made it inclusive of the Jews of Madīnah and the Christians of Najrān, guaranteeing to them their identity and their religious, social, and cultural institutions. History knows of no other written constitution that has honored the minorities as the constitution of the Islamic state has done. The constitution of Madīnah has been in force in the various Islamic states for fourteen centuries and has resisted dictators and revolutions of all kinds – including Genghis Khān and Hulagu!

The *ummah* then is a world order in addition to being a social order. It is the basis of Islamic civilization, its *sine qua non*. In their representation of human reason in the person and career of Ḥayy ibn Yaqẓān, philosophers had discovered that Ḥayy had by his own effort grown to the point of discovering the truth of Islam, and of

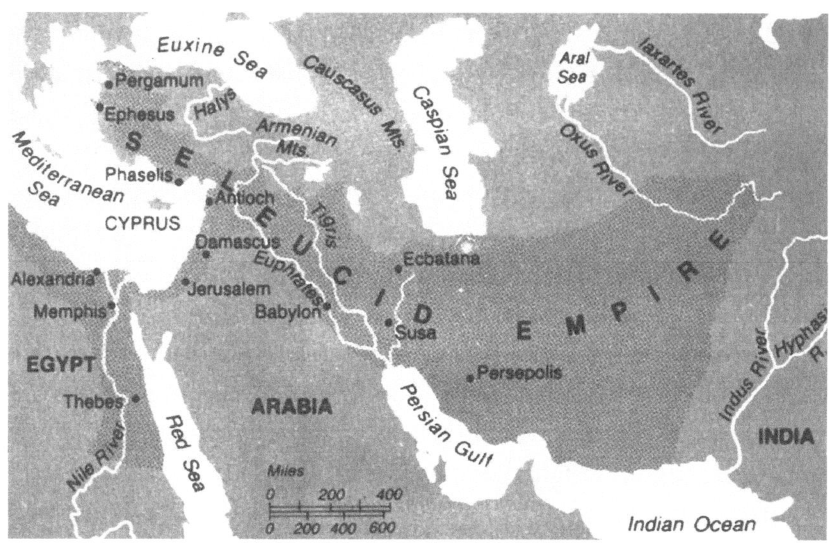

The Seleuci Empire.

tawḥīd, its essence. But having done so, Ḥayy had to invent or discover the *ummah*. He therefore made for himself a canoe out of a hollowed trunk and set forth on the unknown ocean, to discover the *ummah* without which all of his knowledge would not cohere with the truth.

Tawḥīd is, in short, *ummatism*.

TAWḤĪD AS FIRST PRINCIPLE OF AESTHETICS. *Tawḥīd* means to exclude the Godhead from the whole realm of nature. Everything that is in or of creation is a creature, nontranscendent, subject to the laws of space and time. Nothing of it can be God or godly in any sense, especially the ontological which *tawḥīd*, as the essence of monotheism, denies. God is the totally other than creation, totally other than nature, and hence, transcendent. He is the only transcendent being. *Tawḥīd* further asserts that nothing is like unto Him,[44] and hence, that nothing in creation can be a likeness or symbol for God, nothing can represent Him. Indeed, He is by definition beyond representation. God is He Whom no aesthetic intuition whatever is possible.

By aesthetic experience is meant the experience through the senses, of an a priori, metanatural essence that acts as the normative principle of the object beheld. It is what the object ought to be. The nearer the visible object is to that essence, the more beautiful it is. In the case of living nature, of plant, animal, and especially man, the beautiful is that which comes as close to the a priori essence as possible, so that whoever is capable of judging would be right in holding that in the aesthetic object nature has articulated itself eloquently, clearly; that the beautiful object is what nature meant to say, as it does so rarely among its thousand-and-one shortcomings. Art is the process of discovering within nature that metanatural essence and representing it in visible form. Evidently, art is not the imitation of created nature; nor is it the sensory representation of *natura naturata*, the objects whose "naturing" or natural reality is complete. A photographic representation may be valuable for illustration or documentation, for the establishment of identity. As a work of art, it is worthless. Art is the reading in nature of an essence that is non-nature, and the giving to that essence of the visible form that is proper to it.

As it has been defined and analyzed so far, art is necessarily the presumption to find in nature that which is not of it. But that which is not of nature is transcendent; and only that which is divine qualifies for this status. Moreover, since the a priori essence which is the object of aesthetic appreciation is normative and beautiful, man's emotions are especially affected by it. That is why humans love the beautiful and are determined by it. Where they see the beautiful in human nature, the a priori metanatural essence is humanness idealized to a transcendent degree.

The exquisite prayer hall of the Asy-Syakirin Mosque in the heart of Kuala Lumpur, Malaysia.

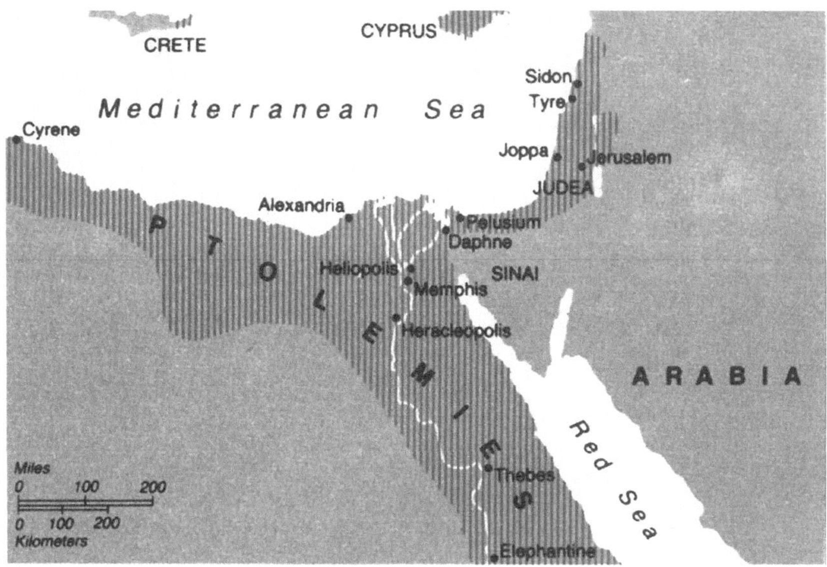

The Ptolemaic State.

This is exactly what the Greeks called *apotheosis*, or the transfiguration of a human into divinity. Humans are particularly prone to adore such transfigured humans and regard them as gods. Modern Western man has little tolerance for any deity as far as metaphysics is concerned. But as far as ethics and conduct are concerned, the "gods" that he creates out of his idealization of human passions and tendencies are the real determinants of his action.

This explains why among the ancient Greeks the arts of representing the gods as apotheoses of human elements, qualities, or passions, visually as in sculpture and imaginatively as in poetry and drama, were the foremost aesthetic pursuits. The objects they represented – the gods – were beautiful because they were idealizations of what human nature ought to be. Their beauty did not hide the innate conflict of each with the other gods, precisely because each was the real object of nature absolutized to its divine, supernatural level.

It was only in Rome, the theater of Greek decadence, that the supreme Greek art of sculpture degenerated into realistic, empirical

The Blue Mosque, Istanbul, Turkey.

portraiture of the various emperors. Even there, however, this would not have been possible without the deification of the emperor. In Greece, where the theory remained pure for centuries, the art of drama developed alongside that of sculpture precisely in order to represent the eternal conflicts of the gods with one another by means of an unfolding of a series of events in which the characters were involved. The overall purpose was the representation of their individual characters which the spectators knew were human, all too human, but which were the source of immense delight. If the dramatic events unfolding before their eyes led to a tragic end, this was regarded as necessary and innate. Its necessity removed its sting and through catharsis it helped remove from them the guilt they felt at their immoral affirmations and pursuits. That is why the art of tragedy, born and perfected in Greece, was the apex of the literary arts as well as of all the humanities. In a rare statement of truth, the Orientalist G. E. von Grunebaum said that Islam had no figurative arts (sculpture, painting, and drama) because it is free of any gods incarnated or immanent in nature, gods whose activities conflict with one another or with evil.[45] Von Grunebaum meant it as a reproach to Islam, though it is in reality Islam's prime distinction. For it is the unique glory of Islam that it is absolutely free of idolatry, of the mistaking of the creature for the Creator. However, the statement remains true; for it shows the intimate relation between the figurative arts, the pagan religions of antiquity, and the incarnational theology of the West.

The Jews had previously asserted that the transcendence of God precluded any making of "graven images," and committed themselves, in obedience to that divine commandment, to a whole history of near total withdrawal from any visual art.[46] They produced some minor works only under the influence of Egypt, Greece and Rome, and Christendom. In modern times, especially since their emancipation under Napoleon and assimilation into Western culture, they have abjured their original Semitic position for the naturalism of the West.

Great Mosque at Djenne, Mali.

Tawḥīd is not against artistic creativity; nor is it against the enjoyment of beauty. On the contrary, *tawḥīd* blesses the beautiful and promotes it. It sees absolute beauty only in God and in His revealed will or words. Accordingly, it was prone to create a new art befitting its view. Starting from the premise that there is no God but God, the Muslim artist was convinced that nothing in nature may represent or express God. Through stylization, he removed every object as far as possible from nature. Indeed, the object of nature was thereby so far removed from nature that it became almost unrecognizable. In his hand, stylization was a negational instrument by which he said No! to every natural thing, to creation itself. By denying its naturalness altogether, the Muslim artist expressed in visible form the negative judgment that there is no God but God. This *shahādah* (witness) of the Muslim artist is indeed the equivalent of the denial of transcendence in nature.

The Muslim artist did not stop there. His creative breakthrough came when it dawned on him that to express God in a figure of nature is one thing, and to express His inexpressibility in such a figure is another. To realize that God – May He be glorified in His transcendence – is visually inexpressible, is the highest aesthetic objective possible for man. God is the absolute, the sublime. To judge Him unrepresentable by anything in creation is to hold His absoluteness and sublimeness seriously. To behold Him in one's imagination as unlike all that is in creation is to behold Him as "beautiful – unlike any other object that is beautiful." Divine

The Eastern Roman Empire.

Interior of the Prophet's Mosque in Madīnah.

inexpressibility is a divine attribute, whose meaning is infinity, absoluteness, ultimacy or nonconditionedness, limitlessness. The infinite is in every sense the inexpressible.

In pursuit of this line of Islamic thought, the Muslim artist invented the art of decoration and transformed it into the "arabesque," a nondevelopmental design that extends in all directions *ad infinitum*. The arabesque transfigures the object of nature it decorates – whether textile, metal, vase, wall, ceiling, pillar, window, or page of a book – into a weightless, transparent, floating pattern extending infinitely in all directions. The object of nature is not itself but is "trans-substantiated." It has become only a field of vision. Aesthetically, the object of nature has become under the arabesque treatment a window onto the infinite. To behold it as suggestive of infinity is to recognize one of the meanings of transcendence, the only one given – though only negatively – to sensory representation and intuition.

This explains why most of the works of art produced by Muslims were abstract. Even where figures of plants, animals and humans were used, the artist stylized them in such a way as to deny their creatureliness, to deny that any supernatural essence is resident within them. In this endeavor, the Muslim artist was assisted by his

Mosque lamp, Egypt, c. 1360 C.E.

linguistic and literary legacy. To the same end, he developed the Arabic script so as to make of it an infinite arabesque, extending non-developmentally in any direction the calligrapher chooses. The same is true of the Muslim architect whose building is an arabesque in its facade, elevations, skyline, as well as floor plan. *Tawḥīd* is the one denominator common to all artists whose worldview is that of Islam, however geographically or ethnically separate they may be.[47]

NOTES

1. See my refutation of the Orientalists who raise doubt that Islam has an essence or that it is known or knowable, in "The Essence of Religious Experience in Islam," *Numen*, 20 (1973), pp. 186-201.

2. In this regard, *tawḥīd* distinguishes itself from Sufism and some sects of Hinduism, where the reality of the world is dissolved into God, and God becomes the only reality, the only existent. In this view, nothing really exists except God. Everything is an illusion; and its existence is unreal. *Tawḥīd* equally contradicts the ancient Egyptian, Greek, and Taoist views that run in a direction diametrically opposed to that of India. In that view, the Creator's existence is dissolved into that of creation or the world. Whereas Egypt maintained that God is indeed Pharaoh, and the green grass blade rising from earth in the spring, and the Nile River with its water and bed, and the disc of the sun with its warmth and light, Greco-Roman antiquity maintained that God is any aspect of human nature or personality magnified to a degree that places it above nature in one sense but keeps it immanent in nature in another. In either case, the Creator is confused with His creation. Under the influence of its priesthood, Christianity separated itself from *tawḥīd* when it claimed that God incarnated Himself in the body of Jesus and asserted that Jesus is God. It is Islam's unique distinction that it emphasized the ultimate duality and absolute disparity of God and the world, of Creator and creature. By its clear and uncompromising stand in this matter of divine transcendence, Islam became the quintessence of the tradition of Semitic prophecy, occupying the golden mean between Eastern (Indian) exaggerationism, which denies nature, and Western (Greek and Egyptian) exaggerationism, which denies God as other.

3. This principle points to the absolute ontological separation of God and man, to the impossibility of their union through incarnation, deification or fusion. The principle, however, does not deny the possibility of communication between them. In fact, it is inseparable from prophecy, or the communication by God to man of a commandment which man is expected to obey. Nor does it rule out the possibility of communication through intellect or intuition, as when man observes the creatures, ponders their whither and why, and concludes that they must have a creator, designer, and sustainer Who deserves to be heeded. This is the avenue of ideation or reasoning. In the final analysis, it is this principle of ontic separation of God and the world that distinguishes *tawḥīd* from all theories that apotheosize man or humanize God, whether Greek, Roman, Hindu, Buddhist, or Christian.

4. As the verses 3:191 and 23:116 indicate.

5. As contained in the verses 7:15; 10:5; 13:9; 15:29; 25:2; 32:9; 38:72; 41:10; 54:49; 65:3; 75:4, 38; 80:19; 82:7; 87:2-3.

6. Qur'an 17:77; 33:62; 35:43; 48:23; 65:3.

7. Any deed that is done "by nature" is *ipso facto* amoral, deserving neither reward nor punishment. Examples are breathing, digestion, or an act of charity or injustice entered into under coercion. It is completely otherwise with the act entered into in freedom, with the possibility of its author doing or not doing it, or doing some other act beside it.

8. This is attested by the verses that speak of the perfection of God's creation (see notes 4, 5 above), and those that stress man's moral obligation and responsibility. The latter are too numerous to count.

9. This is the meaning implied in the verses that speak of the subservience of creation to man, namely, 13:2; 14:32-33; 16:12, 14; 22:36-37, 65; 29:61; 31:20, 29; 35:13; 38:18; 39:5; 43:13; 45:11-12.

10. As the ubiquitous emphases of moral obligation in the Qur'an indicate.

11. The verses dealing with the Final Judgment are very numerous, and there is no need to cite them all; some examples: man will not be left alone without reckoning (75:36), but will be brought to account by God (88:26, 4:85).

12. God prohibited man from doubting his fellows in 4:156; 6:116, 148; 10:26, 66; 49:12; 53:23, 28.

13. This Greek term has no equivalent in Arabic, which illustrates the difference between the minds behind the two languages. The Greek term refers to an irrational dogma adhered to by the Christian.

14. The philosophers have raised reason above revelation and have given it priority status when judging religious claims. Certainly they are wrong in doing so. The Islamic thinker is certainly capable of defining reason differently and to use his definition as premise of all other claims. The question of validity of either definition may certainly be raised, and we have no doubt regarding the philosophic viability, or reasonableness – nay, superiority! – of the Islamic definition. The definition given here, that rationalism is the rejection of ultimate self-contradiction, has, in addition, the value of continuing the tradition of the righteous fathers.

15. Evidence for this can be found in the verses questioning arbitrary prohibition, e.g., 5:90; 7:13; 66:1, as well as the *uṣūlī* (juristic) principle agreed upon by all that "Nothing is

ḥarām (prohibited) except by a text." Consider also the verse, "God has indeed detailed for you what He has prohibited" (6:119, 153).

16. Qur'an 6:42; 12:109; 13:40; 14:4; 15:9; 16:43; 17:77; 21:7, 25; 23:44; 25:20; 30:47; 37:72; 40:70.

17. Ibid., 4:162; 35:23. "We have sent before you [Muhammad] no prophet but We revealed to him that there is no God other than Me. Adore and serve Me."

18. Ibid., 30:30.

19. Ibid., 94:6.

20. Ibid., 49:6.

21. See below, Chapter 14. [Referring to the original *The Cultural Atlas of Islam*].

22. The natural sciences did not develop until the principle was accepted that natural events constantly follow the same immutable laws. That is precisely what Islam has contributed for the development of natural science among its adherents. Its insistence on the orderliness of the cosmos under God provided the atmosphere necessary for the growth of the scientific spirit. The opposite faith, namely, that nature has no constancy but is the field of action of arbitrary deities incarnated therein, or of magical forces manipulating it, can lead to no science.

23. Unlike history, which studies a particular event and analyzes it into its individual constituents and establishes their mutual relations, the natural sciences are concerned with the general pattern, the universal law applicable to all particulars of a given class, or to all members of a class, or to all classes.

24. The same is true of the social sciences and the humanities where the object is the establishment of the laws governing or determining human behavior, individual or collective.

25. In accordance with the verse, "And I have not created jinn or humans but to worship and serve Me" (Qur'an 51:56).

26. As in ibid., 2:30; 6:165; 10:14.

27. Ibid., 33:72.

28. As in ibid., 15:29; 21:91; 38:72; 66:12.

29. To use the term of St. Augustine.

30. Qur'an 11:7; 18:7; 47:31; 67:2.

31. Ibid., 9:95, 106.

32. Ibid., 99:7-8; 101:6, 11.

33. Ibid., 11:61.

34. Ibid., 2:57, 172; 5:90; 7:31, 159; 20:81; 67:15; 92:10.

35. As God had said in the Qur'an, "You may penetrate the regions of heaven and earth if you can. You will not do so except with power and authority" (55:33).

36. Qur'an 57:27. Indeed, we stand under the divine commandment, "And do not forsake your share of this world" (28:77). God taught humans to pray to Him that they "may be granted advantage in this world as well as in the next" (2:201; 7:156). Moreover, He assured them that He will answer their prayers if they do the good deeds (16:30; 39:10).

37. Qur'an 21:92; 23:53.

38. As *Sūrah Al ʿAṣr* (103) indicates. See also 49:10.

39. Ibid., 3:103.

40. Ibid., 3:110; 5:82; 9:113; 20:54, 128.

41. As God has commanded in the verses 3:32, 132; 4:58; 5:95; 24:54; 47:33; 64:12.

42. As the *ḥadīth* said, quoting the Prophet's farewell sermon on his last pilgrimage. By tripartite consensus we mean the sameness of vision or mind or thinking, the agreement of will or decision and intention, and the agreement of action or human arms.

43. The Prophet likened the Muslims to a well-constructed building whose parts consolidate one another; and to an organic body that reacts in its totality whenever any organ or part of it is attacked.

44. Qur'an 42:11.

45. For further details of this question, see Isma'īl al Fārūqī, "Islam and Art," *Studia Islamica*, 37 (1973), pp. 81-109.

46. I. R. al Fārūqī, "On the Nature of the Religious Work of Art," *Islam and the Modern Age*, 1 (1970), pp. 68-81.

47. For further reading on the relation of *tawḥīd* to the other arts, see below Chapters 19-23 [referring to the original *The Cultural Atlas of Islam*]; and Lois Lamya' al Fārūqī, *Aesthetic Experience and the Islamic Arts*, Islamabad: Hijrah Centenary Committee, 1405/1985.